IMAGES
of America

GENEVA LAKE

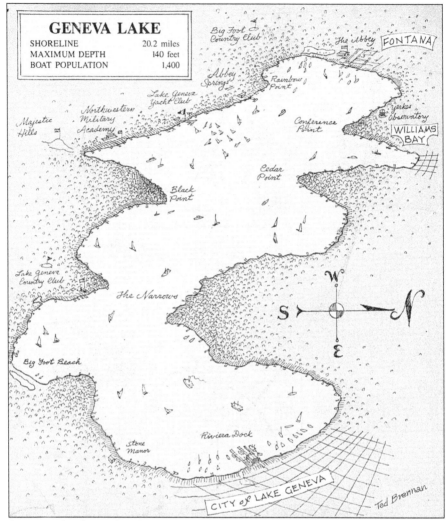

GENEVA LAKE

SHORELINE	20.2 miles
MAXIMUM DEPTH	140 feet
BOAT POPULATION	1,400

Big Foot
Country Club

The Abbey · FONTANA

Abbey
Springs

Rainbow
Point

Lake Geneva
Yacht Club

Northwestern
Military
Academy

Majestic
Hills

Conference
Point

Yerkes
Observatory

WILLIAMS
BAY

Cedar
Point

Black
Point

Lake Geneva
Country Club

The Narrows

Big Foot Beach

Stone
Manor

Riviera Dock

CITY of LAKE GENEVA

—Ted Brennan

Local artist and sailor Frederick "Ted" S. Brennan created this map of Geneva Lake around 1988. After a full career in the industrial design field, Ted turned to his true love of drawing. His legacy lives on through the many images of boats and Geneva Lake that Ted completed over several decades. His wife, Maude, gave permission to use this image in *Lake Geneva in Vintage Postcards*. (Courtesy of Carolyn Hope Smeltzer and Martha Kiefer Cucco.)

ON THE COVER: These girls are having summer fun on Geneva Lake in Williams Bay. Trains, cars, and canoes can be seen in this very active background. The authors hope readers will have as much fun as these girls while reading and viewing Geneva Lake history through family scrapbook photographs and personal memories. This photograph was glued in a family scrapbook with the caption "Lot of Fun!" scrawled in white ink on a black album page. (Courtesy of Curt Carlson.)

IMAGES
of America

GENEVA LAKE

Carolyn Hope Smeltzer and Martha Kiefer Cucco

ARCADIA
PUBLISHING

Published by Arcadia Publishing
Charleston, South Carolina

Library of Congress Control Number: 2014930542

For all general information, please contact Arcadia Publishing:
Telephone 843-853-2070
Fax 843-853-0044
E-mail sales@arcadiapublishing.com
For customer service and orders:
Toll-Free 1-888-313-2665

Visit us on the Internet at www.arcadiapublishing.com

*Carolyn dedicates this book to Bob Kelly. Two decades ago,
Bob introduced her to Geneva Lake living and to golf. Together,
they are still enjoying summer golf in Lake Geneva, Linn,
and Fontana, as well as lake living on Williams Bay.
She also dedicates this book to her Chicago, Geneva Lake area,
and Juno Beach friends as well as her nursing colleagues and family
who make her life meaningful and fun. You know who you are!*

*Martha and Carolyn dedicate this book to the many individuals who
opened up their scrapbooks, took pictures off the wall, searched their
antique trunks, and shared stories of the past. All understood the value
of capturing, sharing, and preserving Geneva Lake history. Without
their contributions, this book would only be a dream, and their unique
memories would have remained silent to the public. Their contributions
created a unique composition of stories and pictures that will be preserved
in this historical scrapbook, Images of America: Geneva Lake.*

CONTENTS

ACKNOWLEDGMENTS

Thanks go to Ann Becker and Ian Spolarich, Barrett Memorial Library; Nancy Krei, Fontana Public Library; Andrea Peterson, Lake Geneva Public Library; Deb Soplanda, Williams Bay Historical Society; and John Halverson, *Lake Geneva Regional News*. Thanks also go to Steve Beers, Patty Birck, Melva Breitenstein, Curt Carlson, Bonnie Cornue, Cathleen Corey, Martha Craven, Bob Kelly, Tim and Donald Kemmett, Peter King, Mary Anne Kirchschlager, Laurie Leitner, Joan and Bart Love, Mary Ann McDermott, Joan Eisner Miller, Jim Moeller, John K. Notz, Jr., Sharon O'Brien, Kay and Mike O'Malley, Jody Pringle, Jim and Daryl Riley, Vince and Nona Sorren, Holly G. Starck, Toby J. Steivang, Carol Swed, and others who shared photographs and stories. A big thank-you goes to Elizabeth "Libby" Probasco Kutchai, whose family, for the past 120 years, cherished photographs, kept scrapbooks, and documented the Rockford Camp history from the beginning, which is chapter one of this book. A special thank-you goes to Allan Button and his wife, Joan Reinert Button. They contributed all but one photograph in chapter three. Allan is the great-grandson of Alexander and Theresa Button, and Joan is the granddaughter of Edward and Martha Reinert. We are convinced Allan and Joan have so much rich family history that they could have written a Geneva Lake book just about their two families' contributions to the area. They contributed to the captions in chapter three with assistance from Wilmur "Bill" Reinert, the youngest son of Edward and Martha Reinert. An extra thank-you goes to Phyllis Janda and the United Church of Christ (Congregational) of Williams Bay. The church board approved use of the majority of pictures shown in chapter four—they said, "we have to share." Without their contributions and Phyllis's facilitation, this chapter would not have been possible. A final thank-you goes to Jacel Egan and Maggie Bullwinkel, who requested and coordinated *Geneva Lake* for Arcadia Publishing. At first, both authors were skeptical, thinking this book would be a duplication of *Lake Geneva in Vintage Postcards*. Quickly, they learned that so many of Geneva Lake's memories and photographs had never been publicly shared and would not be duplicative of their first book, and as they say, "The rest is history."

ABOUT THE AUTHORS

Carolyn Hope Smeltzer, founding partner of Consulting Healthcare Services, a nurse, and a retired PwC partner, is on a "permanent vacation" according to her father—golfing, kayaking, swimming, walking the path, playing bridge, and practicing yoga and tai chi. She is a trustee for Memorial Health Care Medical Center, Chattanooga and Sylvania Franciscan Health Care System, Toledo. She serves on Advocate Healthcare System's Health Outcomes Committee and Christ Medical Center Governing Council. Carolyn is the recipient of Loyola University Chicago's Damen Award and Purdue University's Alumni Award. She, with Fran Vlasses, authored two books, which received international awards—*Ordinary People, Extraordinary Lives, the Stories of Nurses* and *Chicago's Nurse Parade*. Carolyn feels fortunate to share history on three of her passions: nurses, Chicago, and Geneva Lake. All of her books were written in Williams Bay, where her vintage look is riding in her bug convertible listening to Elvis Presley.

Martha Cucco is a real estate broker. Her interest in local history, combined with her knowledge of Geneva Lake, helped to re-create the lake's history in both books. Her hobbies include collecting vintage postcards, photography, sailboat racing, golfing, singing, and hiking the shore path with her golden retriever, Summer. She is active in many volunteer activities around the Geneva Lake area.

Both Carolyn and Martha enjoyed researching and writing their first book about Geneva Lake history, *Lake Geneva in Vintage Postcards*. They are happy to contribute more of the lake's rich history with this book, *Geneva Lake*.

INTRODUCTION

This book is unique. The authors guarantee readers will not have seen the majority of images as most were retrieved from family scrapbooks. Some of the photographs were removed from frames, taken off walls, and searched out of attics or family trunks. In all cases, the owners of the images were very willing and proud to share their photographs, stories, and memorabilia—thus capturing the very soul of the pictures and of the era. They understood by contributing photographs and oral memories to the history of Geneva Lake that they were enhancing "a look back in time" and enriching the reader's pleasure. Many hoped that by sharing their stories, others would begin reminiscing. They believed this book would encourage others to start capturing as well as valuing their own pasts, thus making history more touching, relevant, personal, and definitely preserved.

Geneva Lake focuses on the people, places, pioneers, physical chores, play, and beauty in all areas surrounding the lake: the city of Lake Geneva, Linn Township, and the villages of Fontana and Williams Bay. Chapters one and three hold the images of individuals creating history; chapter two illustrates the community's culture; chapter four highlights work, tools, and perseverance; and chapter five represents what originally attracted individuals to the lake, thus making these communities possible. This book is illustrative of moments in time rather then offering a comprehensive history of Geneva Lake. The book was designed to give the readers an experience that touches their senses in terms of what life was like on Geneva Lake in the past.

Geneva Lake uses individuals' memories to describe an era that otherwise would be forgotten. Oral history is used as a collection and study of historical information about the lake's people, physical chores, pioneers, places, and play. The oral history focuses on families, important events, communities, and everyday life through interviews and handwritten personal notes. These notes were usually found in scrapbooks or on the backs of historical pictures. Sometimes, just looking at the picture alone created the memory and story. This oral history is combined with vintage photographs to make the lake's story come alive.

Interviews were conducted with individuals who either participated in or had connections to others who had lived in a prior Geneva Lake era. Most had friends and family members who told them stories of the history when they were children or young adults. It is hard to argue with their oral history as it is based on memories, passed-down storytelling, feelings, and perceptions.

The oral history presented in this book is coupled with preserved historical photographs and research. Oral history strives to obtain information from different perspectives, and most of these perspectives cannot be found in written research sources but can be recaptured through others who have similar memories. Oral history provides a mechanism to understand and appreciate the past and preserve the heritage for future generations.

The first chapter, "People," is the story about a farmer who leased land to two Rockford, Illinois, families in the late 1800s. These families were not dissimilar from others whose desire was to spend summertime at Geneva Lake because of its cool breezes, lack of diseases, and beauty. This story is used to illustrate the way of summer life and the beginnings of associations that generally had several cottages, a narrow road, and a shared park and pier.

Through the journey of six generations of the Leonard and Probasco families, an appreciation of the work, simplicity, and joy of lake living is demonstrated. Their journeys will also highlight some of the major changes witnessed at the lake. The story with pictures captures how the lake impacted these families as well as how they contributed to their lake's community. The Rockford Camp was like a social experiment on leased land with wooden cottages and a shared kitchen, dining room, lakefront property, and pier. This social experiment lasted over 120 years and spanned six generations.

The second chapter, "Places," focuses on the four communities surrounding the lake in terms of their people, work, play, and peacefulness. The city of Lake Geneva, Linn Township, and villages of Fontana and Williams Bay each had a unique beginning in forming its communities and has unique historical landmarks.

The beginnings of some of the associations will be described, like the Elgin Club and the Englewood Camp (now the Chicago Club) in Linn Township, Belvidere Park in the village of Fontana, and the Congress Club in the village of Williams Bay. In addition, the businesses of Lake Geneva, Yerkes Observatory in Williams Bay, and the school systems in Fontana, Linn, and Lake Geneva will be featured. Each area's unique illustrations will paint a picture of Geneva Lake living in the later 1880s.

In the late 1880s, the city of Lake Geneva was considered the busiest of the four, with many mansions that belonged to wealthy Chicagoans. The shorelines of Williams Bay, Linn, and Fontana were considered more straggling woods country. Lake Geneva was bustling while Williams Bay had only had a dozen homes, a blacksmith, and two stores. The stores were only accessible by horse and buggy. This chapter also focuses on the railroad system that was important to the growth of the each area. Other types of transportation that were used during this era—like horses and buggies, cars, and boats—are illustrated.

The third chapter, "Pioneer Families," focuses on some of the early white settlers and one of the first individuals to build a home in the area he named Button's Bay, Alexander Button. This area was considered the heel of the big-foot-shape section of Geneva Lake. Button built many other significant lake buildings from wood, and most are gone today.

Edward Reinert, construction partner of Reinert and Malsch, constructed many significant lake buildings out of brick and stone. Many of these buildings with their beautiful long-lasting structures are still standing, including the Lake Geneva Country Club and Horticultural Hall. Button's great-grandson Allan married Reinert's granddaughter Joan.

The fourth chapter, "Physical Chores," captures the work that was required to maintain the cottages, estates, fields, communities, and lifestyle at the lake. Prosperity made possible through work is illustrated through numerous pictures highlighting work tools. The construction of Westgate estate in Fontana is also illustrated. This chapter is unique, since everyday work usually is not captured in pictures found in books about Geneva Lake. The photographs are of servants, homemakers, farmers, or churchgoers who were fundraising.

Geneva Lake's last chapter, "Playfulness and Peacefulness," illustrates how people and families spent their time at the lake. It describes the activities of lake living along with the beauty. Photographs in this section really depict the dress, fun, and formality of the era.

This chapter demonstrates the lake's rich history of "things to do" that still exists today: walking the shore path (originally an Indian walkway), swimming, sailing, riding in wooden boats, golfing, sunbathing, fishing in all seasons, iceboating, and skiing. Of course, there are photographs of individuals, families, and friends just relaxing, reading, or reflecting in this peaceful lake environment.

This last chapter truly illustrates why families moved or visited the lake on a regular basis, and why many families stayed connected to the lake for generations. In combination, the chapters provide a rich personal history of lake living in the past that paved the way for lake living today.

One

PEOPLE
TWO FAMILIES, ONE FARMER, SIX GENERATIONS, AND SCRAPBOOKS

Rockford Camp was created on leased farmer's land in 1888. It originated with a handshake between a farmer, Joseph Stam, the landowner since 1884, and two Rockford, Illinois, men.

Josiah Sloan "J.S." Leonard relocated from Syracuse, New York, to Rockford in the 1880s and was missing the Finger Lakes when he discovered Geneva Lake. Leonard, along with his Rockford friend Milton Brown, decided Geneva Lake was a place they wanted to frequent on weekends *60 mile drive by horse + buggy or mayb R.R.* and have their families live in the summer.

During Leonard's normal shore path walk, he noticed the construction of the YMCA Camp. Leonard and Brown decided to lease Stam's "useless lakefront property" close to the campus, giving their families access to church services and activities.

Tents were erected with wooden floors, and canvas ceilings stretched over beams. A primitive horse-and-buggy barn housed a shared kitchen and dining room. The outhouses and icehouse were behind the tents. Collie Spring was used for drinking water.

This was the start of Rockford Camp and of summer lake life that has thrived for over 12 decades and six generations. Stam died in 1907, and his daughter Mrs. Romare sold her half of the property to the Eleanor Camp. His son created a 20-year lease on his property. Eight families lived in Rockford Camp, including the Probascos, whose son married one of Leonard's daughters, Charlotte.

By the 1940s, life changed: Tallow candles were replaced by electricity, the icehouse was dismantled, children no longer argued about walking to Stam's farm for milk because milk was refrigerated, stoves replaced the pits of hot, steamed rocks, and in 1921, plumbing moved inside the cottages, reducing the need to bathe in the lake. The grocery boy no longer came to the cottages taking orders since cars made shopping accessible. In 1975, the Rockford Camp property was sold.

Elizabeth "Libby" Probasco Kutchai, great-granddaughter of J.S. Leonard and W.B. Probasco, and granddaughter of Bill and Charlotte Leonard Probasco, still spends summers in one of the Rockford Camp cottages. Her classic non-winterized cottage that does not have a foundation but does have a screened-in porch represents Rockford Camp and the way it was.

Rockford Camp has been known as Stam's Woods and Dartmouth Woods. Its location was between the YMCA Camp and Eleanor Camp. The property was discovered during one of J.S. Leonard's shore path walks. It was desirable because of water access and camp activities that were shore-path accessible for his families. (Courtesy of Elizabeth Probasco Kutchai.)

Rockford Camp tents had an outhouse back from the lakefront, and their drinking water came from Collie Spring. As Pi Miller remembered, she grimaced whenever the adults asked their guests if they wanted more water because if the answer was yes, the children were sent walking to fetch the springwater. (Courtesy of Elizabeth Probasco Kutchai.)

Great memories include the grocery store boy coming down the hill first thing in the mornings to take orders and delivering the food later that day, the icehouse behind the camp keeping the food cold, and the Rockford Camp mail delivery to the YMCA Camp's post office. (Courtesy of Elizabeth Probasco Kutchai.)

The first cottage only had a couple of bedrooms and a porch. The kitchens and outhouses were detached. After 1921, the cottages had kitchens and bathrooms with showers. Before indoor plumbing and water lines, the lake and a bar of soap were considered the bathing room. (Courtesy of Elizabeth Probasco Kutchai.)

Coming to Lake Geneva meant driving on back roads, and there was always at least one flat tire. Dr. Ruth, J.S. Leonard's youngest daughter, born in 1890, drove fast and once received a speeding ticket in Capron. After this incident, she always pushed her car through the town to avoid another ticket. (Courtesy of Elizabeth Probasco Kutchai.)

Charlotte Leonard (one of the founder's daughters), Bill Probasco, and Bess Miller were Rockford Camp friends. Charlotte, one of six children, started coming to the lake at age two. She married Bill and had two sons, Jack and Lewis. Bess remained her best friend for life. (Courtesy of Elizabeth Probasco Kutchai.)

Charlotte Leonard Probasco's swing was next to the Eleanor Camp. She spent hours swinging all of her grandchildren. Rockford Camp was known for simple lake living. If a family bought new china, furniture, or other belongings for their Rockford home, the old ones went to the lake cottage. (Courtesy of Elizabeth Probasco Kutchai.)

Charlotte did not cook. At noon, she took her grandchildren to Lee's for hot lunches and served sandwiches for dinner. The children usually would picnic with their sandwiches at the pier or in the woods. Other times, a group of neighbors would cook meat in an outdoor hot-stone pit. (Courtesy of Elizabeth Probasco Kutchai.)

Lake living provided relaxation from individuals' weekday jobs. Families and neighbors provided their own entertainment. Music created adult gatherings, and children performed plays. Picnics and card games were numerous. Shore path walks and water activities were part of everyday life. (Courtesy of Elizabeth Probasco Kutchai.)

There were only six piers for 10 eventual cottages in the Rockford camp. When a Probasco grandchild could swim between two piers, he or she received a dollar from Grandmother Charlotte and no longer had to swim with an adult watching from the pier. All grandchildren were motivated to pass the swimming test. (Courtesy of Elizabeth Probasco Kutchai.)

14

A woman before her time, Dr. Ruth liked to have fun and drive fast. She owned one of the first Chris-Craft boats, had a pilot's license, and practiced medicine in the United States and China. She hosted Rockford Camp's only porch happy hour each evening at 4:00 p.m. sharp. (Courtesy of Elizabeth Probasco Kutchai.)

This Rockford Camp lady is beginning a high dive from the pier. When the families first arrived at the lake, the children were only allowed to stay on the pier for 20-minute intervals. Swimming was not allowed on Sundays. One Sunday, the Probasco boys went swimming and a neighbor called them evil. (Courtesy of Elizabeth Probasco Kutchai.)

The Leonard family of Rockford Camp had a sailboat. Bill Rayner, J.S Leonard's grandson, charged the Eleanor Camp ladies 25¢ a ride. Eventually, one of the ladies, Roberta, was not charged for her ride—she later became his wife. (Courtesy of Elizabeth Probasco Kutchai.)

Charlotte Leonard and her husband, Bill Probasco, canoed in the evenings. Canoeing was a way of lake life, and children learned rowing at a young age. Charlotte named her "wood ribbed fiber canvas covered row boat" CERES after her five grandchildren, Charlotte, Elizabeth "Libby," Ralph, Eddie, and Susan. (Courtesy of Elizabeth Probasco Kutchai.)

Ten cottages were in the camp until Pi (Mary Louise) donated one, the Miller Cottage, to Wesley Woods. She moved her cottage when the land was sold. Pi, called "sweetie pie" by her father, spent 93 summers at the lake. Pi is in her canoe here as a young adult (and is seen later in life in the image at the bottom of this page). (Courtesy of Elizabeth Probasco Kutchai.)

There were no secrets in Rockford Camp. Conversations were plentiful in the rowboats, on the pier, and from the porch. Walls in the cottages did not reach the ceilings, providing cross ventilation and reducing privacy. One night, Libby—Charlotte's granddaughter—heard a top- secret discussion about submarines at Amour Research. (Courtesy of Elizabeth Probasco Kutchai.)

Jack and Lewis Probasco were from a family of accomplished swimmers. The Rockford Camp provided lifeguards and swim teachers for all Geneva Lake beaches. Pictured is Jack Probasco, lifeguard, in the 1920s. The brothers spent every summer at the lake, missing only the years of World War II. (Courtesy of Elizabeth Probasco Kutchai.)

Lewis "Lewie" Probasco, a lawyer, always wanted to be a flying trapeze artist. He was a skilled gymnast. During the Depression, he closed his office for three weeks and joined the circus. After the 1970 sale of the Rockford Camp, he moved to the Congress Club. Lewis was an early riser. His routine was to get up at 5:00 a.m., drive to Lake Geneva to get the *Chicago Tribune*, and have breakfast at the Keg Room in Williams Bay, where he was fondly known as "Luigi." His brother Jack, a physician, moved into Ruth's Rockford Camp cottage. (Courtesy of Elizabeth Probasco Kutchai.)

When Pi, as a child, asked for a Fourth of July picnic, her parent's replied, "Okay, if you organize it." Pi initiated the first annual Fourth of July Rockford Camp picnic, which became a 75-year tradition. After her cottage was moved, Pi lived behind the Rockford Camp. This photograph shows the back of the camp. (Courtesy of Peter King.)

Cathleen Eunice Stephen is on a tree limb at the Eleanor Camp in 1930. This camp was created to give ladies a chaperoned camping experience. It ceased to exist when women had other opportunities. It became Wesley Woods, the location Pi moved her cottage to when the Rockford property was sold. (Courtesy of Cathleen Corey.)

Rockford Camp on the shoreline provides a spot of beauty and relaxation, especially with a full moon shining on the lake. Libby Probasco Kutchai, whose great-grandparents were both Leonards and Probascos, initiated a Rockford Camp tradition of "port wine on the pier with a full moon." (Courtesy of Elizabeth Probasco Kutchai.)

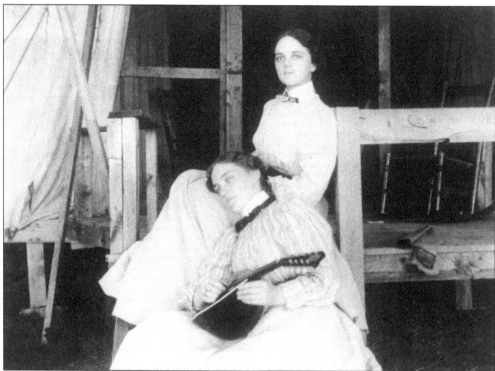

In the summer of 2010, the Rockford Camp (Dartmouth Woods) celebrated 120 years of existence, 120 years of the Leonard family being at the lake, the 100-year anniversary of Ruth's cottage, and the 75th year of the traditional Fourth of July Rockford Camp picnic. Louise and Harriet Leonard are pictured here. (Courtesy of Elizabeth Probasco Kutchai.)

Two

PLACES
CITY OF LAKE GENEVA, LINN TOWNSHIP, VILLAGES OF FONTANA AND WILLIAMS BAY

This chapter focuses on the communities surrounding Geneva Lake. It illustrates associations as well as highlights some of the unique historical buildings, churches, camps, estates, and schools. Yerkes Observatory, businesses, and the railroad are featured.

The Elgin Club was the first of its kind on Geneva Lake. Cottages owned by families from the same location were built around a central dining clubhouse with a common kitchen. Many associations followed the same model—places like Belvidere Park, Congress Club, and Englewood Camp.

Elgin, Illinois, and Lake Geneva, Wisconsin, were connected with a railway from 1856 to 1860. Elgin men developed a fishing lakeside camp. After a storm in 1874, the men decided they wanted to replace tents with cottages. They bought 16 acres of land with 1,450 feet of lakefront in Linn Township from John Wycoff for $400. The plan was to have 10 cottages, but 20 were built because of the venture's popularity.

Belvidere, Illinois, residents were the first charter members of Belvidere Park in Fontana, which was 36 miles by horse and buggy. The first association meeting minutes were recorded in 1875. In 1904, all 18 cottages, on common land, used outdoor toilets and springhouses, which became spring boxes for keeping their food cold.

The Englewood Camp, now the Chicago Club, was created on 17 acres with tents and a cookhouse. It had a dining hall with fireplaces at each end of the building. Cottage houses were built in 1886 with a spring across the road for water. The cost of the land was $8 per acre.

The Congress Club in Williams Bay, established in 1882, had the financial means to deliberate who joined and how they would live. Wealthy businessmen who were neighbors on Congress Street in Chicago, Illinois, formed this association. They had already established a Chicago Congress Club in 1876 for private parties, dancing, fellowship, and theatrical performances.

These association beginnings provide an illustration of how communities started in the Geneva Lake area. It highlights the work of men and women in building their communities while raising their families.

The earliest inhabitants of Geneva Lake, around 1000 BC, were Oneota Indians. They built mounds in Williams Bay, used bows and arrows, and practiced agriculture. These Mound Builders were part of the Aztalan Mississippian culture, which was centered at Cahokia, in modern-day Illinois. (Courtesy of Big Foot Country Club, Melva Breitenstein.)

The Potawatomi were the next Indians inhabiting Geneva Lake. Their main camp was at Fontana. The Potawatomi Indians' lodges had a circular dome built upon arched poles with reed mats for the sides, a slab of bark for the roof, and a fire pit in the center. Skins and furs hung on the interior. (Courtesy of Big Foot Country Club, Melva Breitenstein.)

Seven sacred pools marked a site for the Potawatomi tribe to perform ceremonies. Sprinkling tobacco on the waters was a form of worship believed to add prosperity to their tribe. The Indians still are able to perform ceremonies at the sacred ponds on the Big Foot Country Club golf course in Fontana. (Courtesy of Big Foot Country Club, Melva Breitenstein.)

The Potawatomi tribe settled the area in the mid-1600s. The United States Army removed Chief Big Foot and his tribe in 1836 following the Black Hawk War of 1831–1832 and the treaty agreement of 1833. Chief Big Foot's great-grandson Kahquados is pictured with George Featherstone in Fontana Park to celebrate its centennial. (Courtesy of Barrett Memorial Library and the Fontana Public Library.)

Colonel Kinzie and his companions passed through Fontana in 1831 while traveling from Chicago Fort Dearborn to Fort Winnebago near the Fox and Wisconsin River portage. This is when they came upon Geneva Lake. This area was not on a river or lake roadway, so Geneva Lake was previously undiscovered by white men. This photograph shows an unrelated family in front of Congress Point. (Courtesy of the United Church of Christ (Congregational) of Williams Bay, Phyllis Janda.)

John Brink, a government surveyor, laid claim to the waterfall power and adjacent land at the White River outlet 1835. He named the lake after his home in Geneva, New York. In 1856, it was incorporated into a village, and in 1886, it became a city. Lake Geneva, however, is mostly referred to as the town of Lake Geneva or just Lake Geneva. This image reflects how families traveled. (Courtesy of Allan Button and Joan Reinert Button.)

In 1836, Christopher Payne was one of the white first settlers. Payne relocated to Lake Como after there was a dispute over his land ownership. He had built a dam and mill. Lake Como was originally a wetland for Geneva Lake, which was formed by a glacier. This photograph illustrates travel during this era. (Courtesy of Donald Kemmett.)

Farmers were the settlers after the Indians left the area. They bought land for approximately 1.25¢ an acre. The lakeshore was not considered valuable or useful because of the many trees. It could not be used for planting or grazing. The farmers did their shopping in the towns of Lake Geneva and Delavan. (Courtesy of Curt Carlson.)

The Irish came to the area to be construction workers for the Wisconsin Central Railroad Company. The plan was to build a railway from Genoa Junction through the towns of Geneva, Elkhorn, and Whitewater. The railway was never completed; the Irish, however, stayed. The Williams Bay depot is featured here. (Courtesy of Jim Moeller.)

The first train service came to the area in the 1850s and was from Elgin, Illinois. It lasted only four years. Later, the Chicago & North Western Railway provided services between Chicago, Lake Geneva, and Williams Bay. Here are girls riding the train in Williams Bay. (Courtesy of Curt Carlson.)

In 1901, the Chicago, Milwaukee & St. Paul Railway connected Chicago and Janesville and passed the edge of a town that housed the Linn Township's police and town offices. The railroad president's daughter was riding the train and reading *The Prisoner of Zenda*. Thus, the town was named Zenda. (Courtesy of Curt Carlson.)

The Northwest Pacific Line railroad was established in 1871 from Chicago to Lake Geneva and extended to Williams Bay in 1888. This train line made Williams Bay an ideal location for the Congress Club, recreational camps, religious camps, summer cottages, and estates. (Courtesy of Curt Carlson.)

Fontana means "fountain" in Italian. Sharon and Walworth were all organized under the name Fontana in 1839. Fontana remained unincorporated as a part of the town of Walworth until 1924. Fontana's first settlers were the Van Slyke family in 1836. (Courtesy Donald Kemmett.)

Williams Bay was settled in 1836 and named after Capt. Israel Williams, one of the area's first white settlers. He was a member of the 5th Infantry of the 2nd Brigade of the Massachusetts Militia and became captain in 1825. This photograph was taken next to the Williams Bay 70-foot-diameter train turntable, which was installed in 1892 because Williams Bay was the end of the line. (Courtesy of Curt Carlson.)

Linn Township lies on both the north and south shores of Geneva Lake. John Powers, a native of Maine, built the first house in 1837. Linn was established in 1844, four years before Wisconsin became a state. The town was named for Dr. Lewis Field Linn of Missouri. This photograph is interesting because of the different modes of transportation on the road at the same time. (Courtesy of Holly G. Starck.)

In 1888, Black Point, a 20-room Queen Anne residence, was built for $20,000. Chicago beer baron Conrad Seipp enjoyed his home until his death, just two years later in 1890. Four generations of his descendants enjoyed summers on the eight-acre property with 620 feet of shoreline for decades. The Black Point estate is now a Wisconsin Historic Site. (Courtesy of Holly G. Starck.)

Williams Bay had many recreational facilities. Wisconsin's first summer stock theater, the Belfry, was established in the early 1930s. Paul Newman and Harrison Ford started their acting careers in this theater. Ford was a handyman in between plays and built his own stages. Pictured here are Alvin Johnson and Dyrness, who lived in Williams Bay. (Courtesy of Curt Carlson.)

Irene Dave and Earl Moeller
Cadillac 1914-15

Irene, Dave, and Earl Moeller are seen here with their 1914–1915 Cadillac. At the time, cars did not have it easy with unpaved, gravel or dirt roads. Dave's son Jim Moeller was the first to give his scrapbook photographs for this book. Jim died on December 18, 2013, while this book was being produced. His family said scrapbooking and history were his passions. Note the scrapbooking label on this image. (Courtesy of Jim Moeller.)

30

Martin Nohelty moved to work on the railways after his parents died from the potato famine in Galway, Ireland. He met and married Catherine Nolan from Delavan in 1860. She was two when her family moved from Galway to Delavan. They had nine children. Pictured is one of their grandchildren, Katherine (right rear of automobile). She was the daughter of Alice Boyce Nohelty (Donegal, Ireland) and John Nohelty (Lake Geneva). (Courtesy of Mary Ann McDermott.)

The Irish worshiped at St. Francis de Sales Catholic Church in Lake Geneva. The Irish women wanted a "day off for the Lord," according Charlotte Best Peterson, a past local teacher, Lake Geneva town board member and chairperson of the town planning commission. They went to the church farthest from their homes so they could have an "all-day Sunday affair." The Irish at this time were noted as "laborers" and only recognized silently for their work. The majority of Irish from this era are buried and have tombs in St. Francis de Sales Cemetery. This is where Katherine Noherty's grandparents are buried. She is pictured (left) with an unidentified friend. (Courtesy of Mary Ann McDermott.)

Regardless of whether they were living in tents, cottages, inns, or mansions, Geneva Lake was becoming the place for families to enjoy themselves in the later 1800s. Individuals were creating associations with their neighbors from home, naming them after their hometowns. This row of homes is in Fontana. (Courtesy of Fontana Public Library.)

After the Great Chicago Fire in 1871, Chicagoans were rebuilding their city homes, constructing their Geneva Lake estates, and investing in Wisconsin's farmland. Shelton Sturges of Maple Lawn purchased a farm on McDonald Road. The Crane family owned a farm and hunting lodge. This property is the Hazeldore estate. This estate was built in the later 1800s and is located in Fontana. (Courtesy of Kay O'Malley.)

The Emery family first came to Geneva
Lake in the 1870. They originated
in Maine, relocated to Chicago, and
initially spent summers at Trinke
Estates. By 1924, they relocated and
built cottages at Rainbow Point in
Fontana. (Courtesy of Jody Pringle.)

Henry Bates has spent every summer at
the lake since birth except during his
World War II service years. He celebrated
his 90th birthday at Lake Geneva
Country Club in the summer of 2012.
Henry is pictured with Nancy Pollock,
his second cousin and life-long friend, at
Rainbow Point. (Courtesy of Jody Pringle.)

The March 18, 1882, Congress Club minutes indicate that monies were appropriated for building their clubhouse and two homes. The Healy home was one of the first built. Members whose homes were under construction lived in the clubhouse's upstairs apartments. By 1887, all 10 homes had been erected in the Congress Club. (Courtesy of Carol Swed.)

Congress Club families pose in front of house No. 9 and are, starting in the back row, Mr. and Mrs. Gray Gertrude Post, Helen Jerrems, Mrs. Sears, Mrs. Taylor, Dr. Shears, Mr. Taylor, Mr. Meacham, Mr. Post, Mr. Harvey Weeks, Mrs. Jerrems, Mrs. Hill, Mrs. Post, Mrs. Meacham, the Meacham boy, and the two Taylor boys. (Courtesy of Carol Swed.)

Kitchens were omitted from the Congress Club's homes. The clubhouse was a common cooking and dining facility. If a member put a kitchen in his home, the member's family was no longer allowed to dine in the clubhouse. Pictured are John Bush, a friend, and two children in front of the vegetable garden. (Courtesy of Carol Swed.)

Other Congress Club buildings included the billiard hall that housed chauffeurs and boat captains, the icehouse, and the bowling alley. Many of these buildings were later torn down and the lumber was used for garages. Pictured here is a child in front of the laundry building. (Courtesy of Carol Swed.)

Early founders of the Illinois nonprofit Congress Club were George Parker, Charles Post, Patrick Healy, and Harvey Weeks. They had searched for a relaxing lake environment that could provide the same social activities they had in Chicago. Mrs. William Jackson, daughter of Harvey Weeks, is pictured second from the right. (Courtesy Carol Swed.)

Mrs. Jackson, top row, left, and daughter of Harvey Weeks (a founding member of Congress Club), poses with other girls. She lived in house No. 8 from 1920 until 1963. The Congress Club houses originally were in a line, but with rumors of the Indians returning, they were moved into a protective semicircle. (Courtesy of Carol Swed.)

In 1885, Chas Dodge received $100 for closing the Congress Club grounds for the winter. This included removing the piers, filling the icehouse, and removing snow from the porches. The girls pictured here are posing in front of the lake at the Congress Club. (Courtesy of Carol Swed.)

Patrick Healy's family, from the Lyon and Healy Music Company, was expanding, so he built down the road from the Congress Club. His son, Marquette A., built an estate adjacent to his father's property. Towering Elms, originally Wood Brook, was sold in 1933 to the Niehoff family. This home reportedly has the only Steinway piano that was never sold for retail. (Courtesy of Mary Anne Kirchschlager.)

In 1904, all 18 Belvidere Park cottages had outdoor toilets and spring boxes for keeping their food cool. A hand-painted sign reading "Belvidere Park" was hung up in 1906, and in 1916, electricity was introduced to the association. (Courtesy of Sharon O'Brien.)

Tradesmen would come by horse and buggy in the morning to Belvidere Park to take orders for meat and groceries. Carriages or boats would deliver the ordered goods later in the afternoon. A Belvidere Park cottage is pictured. (Courtesy of Sharon O'Brien.)

These Belvidere Park residents are shown having fun. Horses and buggies were first used for travel to Belvidere Park, then trains. Individuals could board the North Western line to Caledonia, have lunch, catch the Harvard train, and then board another train to the lake. Their trunks were transported by rowboat while they walked the shore path to reach their cottages. (Courtesy of Sharon O'Brien.)

Names were drawn out of a hat to determine where Belvidere lot owners could erect their tents or cottages, several of which are pictured here. Their total 1877 property assessment was approximately $113, and taxes were $9. It is in Belvidere Park where the first meeting was held to establish Big Foot Country Club. (Courtesy of Patty Birck.)

The Englewood Camp, made up of 17 acres of land and now named the Chicago Club, started with tents and a cookhouse in 1858. It had a miniature rail track for horses to pull a cart filled with boat-delivered goods from the lakeside to the top of the hill cottages. The first residents were from the Englewood neighborhood in Chicago, Illinois. This photograph is from *Picturesque Lake Geneva*, published by Wisconsin Transportation Company. (Courtesy of Bob Kelly.)

This photograph was taken in front of the Englewood Camp, now the Chicago Club. The cookhouse was built away from the lake to protect the homes from a potential fire. Servants were housed in space above the cookhouse. The original cookhouse needed painting, but the homeowners did not want the expense, so it was razed. In 1929, the first kitchen was put in one of the main Englewood Camp homes. (Courtesy of Jim and Daryl Riley.)

Linn Township had the first Wisconsin 4-H club, a gristmill, cheese plants, two general stores, a lumberyard, the Northwestern Military and Naval Academy, and a blacksmith shop in 1914. Pictured are families at the Englewood Camp. (Courtesy of Jim and Daryl Riley.)

Many of the settlers in Linn came from Ireland. The first town meeting in Linn was in 1844. In 1845, John Reek, from England, took an active role in starting the school, and the first post office was in Zenda. One-sixth of Linn township is on the shoreline, covering 14 of the 26 lakefront miles. This picture was taken in front of the Englewood Camp, located in Linn Township. (Courtesy of Jim and Daryl Riley.)

Elgin Club homes are noted for their curved porches and views. This is one of the homes in the Elgin Club that is still in its original form, as most have been renovated by different owners. The club originally started with fishing tents in 1872 and the first home was built in 1878. The Craven home was built in 1882 and is owned by Martha Craven, a descendant of the original owner. (Courtesy of Martha Craven.)

The Elgin Club was the first of the associations to be formed, but many followed. The Congress Club, Belvidere Park, Englewood Camp, and Harvard Club were modeled after the Elgin Club. Today, the Elgin Club does not have its primitive cottages, but rather, many are wooden Victorian Lady–style homes. The homes were cozy inside. (Courtesy of Martha Craven.)

William Gooding, Charles Moseley, Alfred Lavoine, and A.H. Smith bought 1,450 feet of north shore lakefront property on a 16-acre lot from owner John Wycoff for $400. The plan was for 10 lots for Elgin, Illinois, families, but because of popularity, the number grew to 20. These residents of the Elgin Club are getting ready for a sail. (Courtesy of Martha Craven.)

When the original clubhouse of the Elgin Club no longer existed, the tradition of camaraderie continued. Residents would gather at their pier or wait for their mail while sharing stories. Instead of dining together, they would gather on their porches for conversation. Ruth is having fun on the pier in this photograph. (Courtesy of Martha Craven.)

Conference Point in Williams Bay was originally Collie Camp, associated with the Congregational church in Delavan. A Collie Camp advertisement stated that reasonable boarding by day or week was offered in a camp with rooms, boats, laundry facilities, milk, and ice. Here, these unidentified little girls are welcoming folks to Williams Bay. (Courtesy of Curt Carlson.)

Gus Johnson had property and a farm in Williams Bay. His children were Helmer, Elsie, Alvin, and Mabel. Elsie never married and was a missionary to the Indians. Helmer took over the Johnson farm after Gus died. Alvin became a carpenter, and Mabel married Herb Blodgett. (Courtesy of Curt Carlson.)

A farmer poses with his child and other men after a hard day's work. Farmers did not value the lakeshore property attached to their farms. The lake property was considered useless for planting and grazing. Farmers therefore leased or sold their shoreline property to those who wanted to live close to the water. (Courtesy of Donald Kemmitt.)

Alvin Johnson was a carpenter who built his own home on Cherry Street in Williams Bay. His daughter Carolyn, Curt Carlson's mother, is photographed here by their home. (Courtesy of Curt Carlson.)

Mr. & Mrs. Alvin Johnson's home on the corner of Cherry and Hill. Carolyn Johnson pictued . 1932

In 1890, astronomer George Ellery Hale learned that the University of Southern California had abandoned its project of creating the world's largest telescope. He and Rainey Harper, president of the University of Chicago, approached Charles Tyson Yerkes to fund his new project, which became Yerkes Observatory in Williams Bay. (Courtesy of Barrett Memorial Library.)

The University of Chicago built Yerkes Observatory with a gift from Charles T. Yerkes on a 53-acre parcel in 1895. Yerkes Observatory was under construction between 1895–1897. It was built in the form of a Roman cross. Two engineers working on the observatory ended up building cottages next to Rockford camp. All used the pier of Rockford Camp. (Courtesy of Holly G. Starck.)

Yerkes Observatory has the largest refractory lens in the world. It was built in Williams Bay to get away from the light and pollution of the city. Henry Ives Cobb was the architect; he also designed a building for the World's Columbian Exposition in Chicago in 1893. (Courtesy of Holly G. Starck.)

Albert Einstein at the Yerkes Observatory

When Albert Einstein was coming to America for the first time, he asked to see two places—Niagara Falls in upstate New York and Yerkes Observatory in Williams Bay, known as the birthplace of modern astrophysics. On May 6, 1921, Einstein (eighth from right) is pictured during his visit to Yerkes Observatory. (Courtesy of Holly G. Starck.)

Carlos Douglass joined his father in the farming, mill, and real estate business. They built the first full-roller grain mill in southern Wisconsin. In 1909, Ruthford Douglass Davis owned the Douglass Mill Company after he returned from his service duties. This is a photograph of Mill Street in the village of Fontana. (Courtesy of Donald Kemmett.)

A store and the post office are visible in the village of Fontana. The train or trolley depot was also located close to the lakefront in Fontana. (Courtesy of Fontana Public Library.)

The village of Fontana was always noted for its parks and meeting places. Porter Park was in the location of the current Buena Vista Club, which celebrated its 100-year anniversary in 2013. There could not be a Wisconsin book without featuring beer, even way back then. (Courtesy of Fontana Public Library.)

These cottages in Glenwood Springs are pictured in 1909. Located in Fontana, Glenwood Springs also had a boat landing, park, and hotel. (Courtesy of Fontana Public Library.)

Burton's large wooden flouring mill was located by the White River. Reinert and Malsch built the Wisconsin Power and Light Company maintenance garage on this property. This historic building is made out of red brick with huge wooden roof trusses and now houses the Lake Geneva Museum. The Geneva Flouring Mill is at right. (Courtesy of Allan Button and Joan Reinert Button.)

Although many businessmen came from Chicago to settle into a summer home in the Geneva Lakes area, local business individuals also emerged in the banking, grocery, restaurant, and hotel industries. This is the meat market on the 700 block of Main Street in Lake Geneva. It was started in 1898 and was called the Host Bros. Market. (Courtesy of T.C. Smith Historic Inn.)

Diamond trucks delivered supplies to
homes as well as building materials to
construction workers. Prior to the lake area
having road access, many cottages and
tents were assembled in Lake Geneva and
carted by horses across the lake's frozen
ice for their final locations. This was true
of the Rockford Camp's original housing.
(Courtesy of Lake Geneva Public Library.)

Sidney Smith was the creator of the Andy
Gump comic strip character in the *Chicago
Tribune*. Sidney died in a car accident
in 1935. Pictured is the Andy Gump
statue with Viola Twist in Flat Iron Park.
Edward Reinert was a friend of both the
Smith and Twist families. (Courtesy of
Allan Button and Joan Reinert Button.)

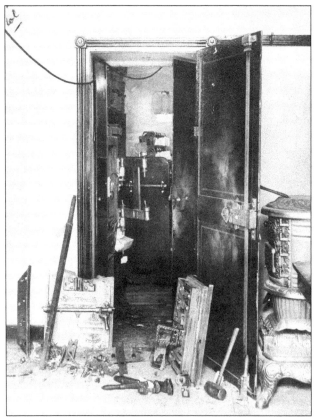

The Walworth Exchange
Bank was the forerunner of
the Walworth State Bank,
founded in 1903. Originally, it
was organized in the parlor of
the Wayside Hotel. The bank
was considered by many to be
one of the safest institutions
in southern Wisconsin, but
nevertheless was robbed and
later burglarized. (Courtesy
of Toby J. Steivang.)

The burglars came in the back
of the bank by prying open the
bank's windows from the alley.
The safe was then destroyed,
and the valuables were stolen.
(Courtesy of Toby J. Steivang.)

Davidson formed the Northwestern Military Academy in 1888, and it moved to Linn Township in 1915. For over a century, the academy provided education rooted in military structure and religious principles to young men. Katherine Nohelty (second from left) is pictured with friends at the academy after her 1918 high school graduation. (Courtesy of Mary Ann McDermott.)

Israel Williams, the founder of Williams Bay, moved to Linn. His home became the Buckhorn Tavern. Israel Jr. became chairman of the town of Linn supervisors in 1847. Pictured is Israel's youngest son, Festus, born in 1832, with Williams Bay's first church in the background—the Scandinavian Church, formerly known as the Free Evangelical Lutheran Church (Courtesy of Barrett Memorial Library.)

William Moeller had the first water taxi service in Williams Bay. Registration for a pier and business were not needed. He just found a spot in the bay, built the pier, and docked Chris-Craft boats for transportation. The Wisconsin Transportation Company located next to his business sold Garwood boats. William was Jim Moeller's grandfather. (Courtesy of Jim Moeller.)

Moeller gave rides around the lake for 25¢. He also provided transportation from the train station in Williams Bay to lake homes. Lightning hit William Moeller with passengers in his transportation boat one summer afternoon. He survived, and no passengers were injured. The Moeller water transportation and speedboat ride company was sold in 1946. (Courtesy of Jim Moeller.)

Williams Bay's library was first located in Mrs. Edward Williams's home. In 1907, Barrett—a Yerkes astronomer—knew Mrs. Sturges was razing her clubhouse and bowling alley. He requested this property be moved to Williams Bay for the library and village meeting place. Pictured here is the Sturgeses' home. (Courtesy of Steve Beers.)

Williams Bay had numerous camps that served the purpose of providing opportunities for those from Chicago to escape the busy city, relax, play sports, take educational classes, and certainly swim, sail, and boat on the lake. Pictured here is the Redins' home on Highway 67. (Courtesy of Curt Carlson.)

Lake Geneva was always a place to celebrate. In the 1800s, the town had its first July Fourth parade. The Diamond Block Supply House float was a small house with a sign that read, "We handle everything you need." It was drawn by horses and decorated with flags. (Courtesy of Allan Button and Joan Reinert Button.)

The tinner's parade float featured drainpipes, a furnace with tinned duct, tinned ceiling sections, and American flags. Tinners walked alongside this float in the parade. (Courtesy of Allan Button and Joan Reinert Button.)

The circus came to town on Main Street in Lake Geneva. Camels are pulling one of the circus wagons. The town buildings are a good illustration of an architectural style that was accomplished with the Reinert's cement block fronts. The faces of the blocks were his specialty. (Courtesy of Allan Button and Joan Reinert Button.)

Elephants and their caretakers are waiting to march in the circus parade. In 1847, two brothers from New York named Mabie came to Delavan and established a winter quarters for their circus animals. In 1891, W.S. Coup developed the P.T. Barnum Circus in Lake Geneva's neighboring town of Delavan. (Courtesy of Allan Button and Joan Reinert Button.)

The 1887–1888 Fontana public school orientation booklet describes the school calendar, the textbooks to be used by different grades, and the cost for non-resident students, which was 25¢ a week. To become a teacher, one only really had to read and write and may not have completed high school. (Courtesy of the Fontana Public Library.)

Children pose in front of the Fontana School house. The school, on the hill, opened in 1860 as a one-room schoolhouse and closed in 1893. In 1870, there were 14 students. Young children were educated in the summer by women, and older ones received schooling in the winter from male teachers. (Courtesy of Fontana Public Library.)

Woods School was built in 1858 to educate the Irish children of the railroad workers. Martin Nohelty exchanged some of his Irish Woods farmland for the Woods School building. He and his wife, Catherine Nolan Nohelty, are pictured in the center of the middle row. Their nine children are, from left to right, (back row) Elizabeth Nohelty Lee, John Edward Nohelty, Ellen Nohelty Croden, Patrick Nohelty, and Katherine "Katy" Nohelty Watson; (middle row) Martin Nohelty and Mike Nohelty; (front row) Sarah Nohelty Ready and Winifred Nohelty Deignan. (Courtesy of Mary Ann McDermott.)

Katherine Nohelty poses in the middle, with Mary McDonald to the left and Sarah Haley to the right. They attended a picnic in front of Woods School right after they finished watching a ball game in 1915. John Edward Nohelty, the eldest child in the family portrait, is the grandfather of Mary Ann McDermott, and Katherine (pictured) is her aunt. (Courtesy of Mary Ann McDermott.)

Assembled here in 1895 are children engaged in active learning at the Fontana School. Oil lamps were used for lighting. The school did not have electricity until 1905. (Courtesy of Donald Kemmett.)

The Lake Geneva High School faculty poses for its annual photograph in 1920. Pictured are, from left to right, (first row) Al Drake, Anna Stewart, Miss Wakeman, Mrs. Perry, Mrs. Piehl, S.M. Mielki; (second row) Mr. Donahue, B.D. Richeson, A. Post, Professor Rood, Mr. Kazmarack, and B.D. Baily. (Courtesy of Allan Button and Joan Reinert Button.)

Ready to take on an opponent, the Lake Geneva High School football team poses before a game in 1920. Albert Reinert is second from the left in the front row. (Courtesy of Allan Button and Joan Reinert Button.)

The 1921 graduating class of Lake Geneva High School assembles for its photograph. The school began in 1895. The city purchased the former Young Women's Seminary as a temporary building until the high school and middle school were built. It was replaced in 1958. Albert Reinert is second from right in the first row. (Courtesy of Allan Button and Joan Reinert Button.)

Fontana Community Church formed in 1886 and became affiliated with the Congregational Church in 1896. In addition, Father Eparch of Sharon started a Catholic mission in 1912, and St. Benedict was founded in 1916. Pictured here are some ladies getting ready to go to church. (Courtesy of the United Church of Christ (Congregational) of Williams Bay, Phyllis Janda.)

This is Fontana's first church, which was built in 1890 on West Main Street. The church structure was moved in 1923. In 1927, it became the east wing of the newly built church on Reid and Kinzie Streets in Fontana. (Courtesy of Donald Kemmett.)

Three

PIONEER FAMILIES
ALEXANDER BUTTON AND
EDWARD REINERT AND
THEIR FAMILIES' INFLUENCE AND
CONTRIBUTIONS TO THE GENEVA LAKE
COMMUNITY

Alexander "A.H." Button, along with his three brothers, walked to Geneva Lake from Chicago. In 1850, he built a home on the southeast side of the lake. He named the area Button's Bay. Born in 1828, Alexander was originally from Floyd, New York, and married Theresa Barker. They had nine children. He was a builder, contractor, schoolteacher, and town clerk in Linn Township for 30 years.

Button was contracted to build the first family summer estate on the east side of the lake called Gypsy Lodge. According to the *Lake Geneva Herald*, "this is the first summer residence on this part of the shore, which is so pretty that it is a wonder that others have not seen it before." Button constructed many now historical frame buildings around the lake, including the dining hall at the YMCA Camp.

Two of Button's sons, Frank and Silas, began Button Brothers Greenhouse when they were asked to plant for Mrs. C.C. Boyles of Sumachs Estate and Prof. David Swing of the Swinghurst Estate in 1884. This was the lake's first greenhouse, heated with a stove and operated for 75 years. Another son, George, was an artistic tinsmith, wood-carver, and cabinet- and furniture maker. His son Charles started an upholstery business, eventually making boat covers and awnings. The business is now owned by Charles's son, Fredrick "Fritz", who also makes racing Skeeter-class iceboats.

Allan Button, son of Charles and great-grandson of Alexander, married Joan Reinert, granddaughter of Edward Reinert. Edward's parents came from Markendorf, Germany, and moved to Lake Geneva in 1885. He met Martha Gartz, a maid for the Arnold family, when he was delivering groceries. They married and had nine children. Edward became an owner and partner of Reinert and Malsch Construction Company. Reinert's historical buildings were made of enduring cement block or brick construction. Some of the buildings included the boathouse of Green Gables; Lake Geneva High School in 1901; Horticultural Hall; Christian Science Church building; rebuilt Lake Geneva Country Club (after the first clubhouse was destroyed by a fire); the underwater foundation for the Riviera; the Wisconsin Power and Light Garage that now houses the Lake Geneva Museum; Mary Stevener Rienhart's (his mother) home at 905 Marshall Street; the Evangelical Luthern Schoolhouse; and Oak Hill Cemetery' office, storage building, and chapel.

Both families left historical landmarks in the Geneva Lake area and contributed significantly to the community.

Alexander Button, pictured here with his wife, Theresa, settled by Geneva Lake in 1850. He built and lived at the "heel" of the big-foot shape of the lake on the southeast corner. As a contractor, he used wood framing to build some of the finest lake estates. Most of his buildings no longer exist. (Courtesy of Allan Button and Joan Reinert Button.)

In the 1850s, A.H. Button was one of the first white men to build on land he named Button's Bay. He built his own home named Shadyside, and as a carpenter and contractor built Gypsy Lodge in 1883. In 1920, the lodge owner, Dr. Peitrowicz, converted it to a guesthouse and restaurant named Sunnycroft Lodge. (Courtesy of Allan Button and Joan Reinert Button.)

Dow was the first owner of Gypsy Lodge, followed by Rumsey, president of the Chicago Board of Trade and Chicago mayor. The third owner, Jones, enlarged the lodge and hosted many parties with his wife, Helen, and her sister Katherine Isham. Eventually, the lodge was named the Button's Bay Inn. (Courtesy of Geneva Inn.)

Alexander and his wife, Theresa, had nine children. The children had talents varying from planting to wood and tin craftsmanship. Alexander himself was a builder, contractor, teacher, and penmanship instructor. In this family picture are, from left to right, (first row) Clara, Alexander, Theresa, and Maybelle; (second row) George, Silas, Ezra, and Frank. (Courtesy of Allan Button and Joan Reinert Button.)

Frank and Silas Button, two of Alexander's sons, were asked by Mrs. C.C. Boyle of Sumachs Estate and Prof. David Swing of Swinghurst Estate to grow plants. A greenhouse was constructed in 1883 that used stove heat. Silas did the greenhouse work, and Frank did the landscaping. (Courtesy of Allan Button and Joan Reinert Button.)

Silas died in 1904, and his wife married Frank Button. Silas's son, Alexander "Pat," his wife, Pearl, and his sister Helen ran the Button Brother's Greenhouse until it closed in the 1960s after a run of 75 years. Pictured are Alexander (the grandson of Alexander, the founding Button settler) and his sister Helen. (Courtesy of Allan Button and Joan Reinert Button.)

George, Alexander Button Sr.'s eldest son, was quite talented and resourceful. Born in 1864, he was an artistic cabinet- and furniture maker, wood-carver, and tinsmith. He is pictured here, third from the left, at Travis and Parshall's Hardware Store. The ceiling is typical of a tinsmith's work. (Courtesy of Allan Button and Joan Reinert Button.)

George's desk side panel displays his talents at woodcarving. The intricate design is his original work. He had a very artistic skill, not only with wood but also with tin. His grandson Allan states, "I am amazed at how broad and varied were the activities of those early generations." (Courtesy of Allan Button and Joan Reinert Button.)

George married Lillie Kinney and they had four children—Lillie May, Mabelle D., Mildred E., and Charles. This photograph is a typical portrait of this generation. (Courtesy of Allan Button and Joan Reinert Button.)

This picture is of George (far left) as a furniture maker. George also owned a carriage repair and upholstering shop. He was very resourceful and did many different types of work in his lifetime. (Courtesy of Allan Button and Joan Reinert Button.)

The home that George designed and built on Curtis Street became the home where his son Charles and Charles's wife, Hazel, raised their family of three sons. The sons were Allan, Frederick "Fritz," and John. Buttons occupied this home until the mid-1980s. (Courtesy of Allan Button and Joan Reinert Button.)

George's son Charles had a desire to be a commercial gardener, selling flowers and vegetables. During the Depression, few had money to buy goods and most planted their own vegetables. He took many jobs to make money. Pictured here in a typical family portrait of the era are George's daughters, son, wife, and mother. (Courtesy of Allan Button and Joan Reinert Button.)

Charles Button, pictured here with Hazel on their wedding day, started reupholstering a couch in an old, rundown flat-roofed wooden storage building. He ran an upholstering shop that became one of the most successful and largest reupholstering businesses in Wisconsin. Charles eventually enlarged his business into making boat covers and awnings. His son Fredrick "Fritz" continued the business. (Courtesy of Allan Button and Joan Reinert Button.)

Charles's business has existed for over six decades. Fritz continues to make boat covers and canopies for specialized boats as well as designing and building fast Skeeter-class iceboats. He has a wood and metal shop, taking after both his father and his grandfather George Button. (Courtesy of Allan Button and Joan Reinert Button.)

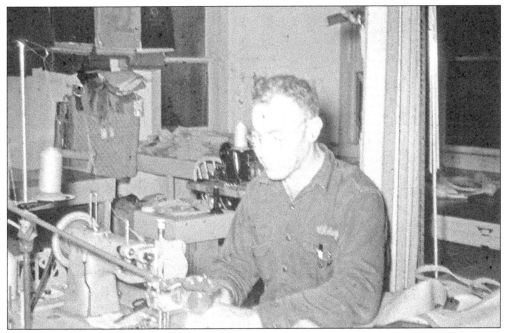

Charles Button's shop is shown here. The original shop was destroyed by fire in 1948. His upholstery business flourished and specialized in custom-fit boat covers, boat interior upholstery, and, later, canvas canopies that protect the boats from rain and sun. (Courtesy of Allan Button and Joan Reinert Button.)

Charles Button and Albert Reinert attended Lake Geneva High School and played in the band in 1920. Charles's grandfather Alexander and Albert's father, Edward, contributed many now historic lake buildings. Charles is second from the left in the front row with a clarinet, and Albert is in the top row on the left end with a baritone horn. They were six years apart in age. (Courtesy of Allan Button and Joan Reinert Button.)

Herman and Mary Reinert, originally from Markendorf, Germany, moved to Lake Geneva in 1885 with their son Edward, who was 13. Edward spent his early years in St. Louis. (Courtesy of Allan Button and Joan Reinert Button.)

Edward, in 1894, built a home and barn on George Street. The road was not paved, and he had a hitching post for horses. The basement was made of dirt, and in autumn he would stock 40 bushels of potatoes and other vegetables for the winter months. (Courtesy of Allan Button and Joan Reinert Button.)

Reinert's barn was behind his home. It was built with three doors. The first, on the left, was for his horses, the second entrance was for the carriage, and the third door was for wood storage. Edward began a construction business and partnered with Malsch and Baumbach in 1906. (Courtesy of Allan Button and Joan Reinert Button.)

Edward married Martha Gartz a year after the completion of his house. He met Martha when he was delivering groceries for the Smith and Lock Grocery Store to the Arnold residence, where Martha was a maid. They raised nine children. Pictured are Edward, Martha, and their daughter Clara. (Courtesy of Allan Button and Joan Reinert Button.)

Here is a Reinert family portrait from 1920. In the photograph are, from left to right, (standing) Gertrude, Edward Jr., Edith, Ralph, Allen, Clara, and Albert; (seated) Martha, Marion, Edward, and Wilbur. (Courtesy of Allan Button and Joan Reinert Button.)

Albert Reinert, one of Edward and Martha's nine children, practices fishing in 1908. Most of the photographs that feature the Button family or the Reinert family are from old family albums, with the pictures actually being described by the ancestors in their own handwriting in white ink on the black album pages. (Courtesy of Allan Button and Joan Reinert Button.)

Albert Reinert could be found working at Arnold's drugstore that was located in Williams Bay. The main store was in the downtown area of Lake Geneva. The drugstore also offered home delivery. (Courtesy of Allan Button and Joan Reinert Button.)

Albert married Evelyn and they drove this car during their honeymoon. Evelyn is shown seated in the car. Albert became the accountant for his father's company and also was a carpenter and designer. (Courtesy of Allan Button and Joan Reinert Button.)

The Reinert and Malsch Construction Company used cement, lime, and masonry supplies. While the company built the present Lake Geneva Country Club in 1915, horses and a wagon were carrying materials across the frozen lake when the ice broke. A skid was formed, the wagon was retrieved, and the horses were saved. (Courtesy of Allan Button and Joan Reinert Button.)

Pictured is the company's cement mixer. Edward developed a system to manufacture a special cement block with the face looking like crushed granite. This block was used for many of the Lake Geneva downtown buildings and is still the facade on some of the older buildings. (Courtesy of Allan Button and Joan Reinert Button.)

Edward served on boards of the school and the Lake Geneva Light and Water Commission. He was a supervisor for the Walworth County Board and was a Third Ward alderman. Edward served as a deacon, financial secretary, treasurer, and trustee of the First Evangelical Lutheran Church. Albert (on the left) is working in the office of Reinert and Malsch. (Courtesy of Allan Button and Joan Reinert Button.)

The crew is shown constructing a farm building and silo. As the dairy business grew, the demand for silos increased. In 1908, the Reinert, Malsch, and Baumbach Company began to manufacture specially designed curved cement block for farm silos and built many between the years 1908 and 1914. (Courtesy of Allan Button and Joan Reinert Button.)

The Pelouze estate, pictured here, demonstrated the Italian influence. Reinert built this as well as his mother's cement-block home and some English-style homes. The company also constructed the historic landmark Horticultural Hall in 1912. In 1915, Mrs. Charles Hutchinson and other lakeshore ladies formed the Lake Geneva Garden Club. (Courtesy of Allan Button and Joan Reinert Button.)

Reinert and Malsch built the Green Gables boathouse (pictured) on the William Wrigley estate, the Evangelical Lutheran School House, the Christian Science Church building, and the champion draft horse barn on the J.J. Mitchell estate. Dan Patch, the famous harness racing horse, stayed in the barn at Ceylon Court from 1901 to 1902. (Courtesy of Allan Button and Joan Reinert Button.)

The Reinert and Malsch's parade float demonstrates the special cement block. The company used cement, lime, and masonry supplies. It manufactured concrete blocks, bricks, and tiles for wells and burial vaults and owned a masonry supply warehouse. It also built the Lake Geneva High School and Middle School. (Courtesy of Allan Button and Joan Reinert Button.)

This parade float of the tinner's trade group features drainpipes. George Button, Allan Button's grandfather, was a tinsmith, and he is third from the left. This float may have been carried by hand, using the pipe rails along the sides. (Courtesy of Allan Button and Joan Reinert Button.)

Allan Button, George's grandson, is in front of the fishing boat with his brother Fritz and his mother, Hazel (Webster) Button. The Reinerts and Buttons were civic leaders and contributed to their communities. Both families constructed significant historic buildings, structures, homes, and businesses that shaped the look and the culture of Lake Geneva. (Courtesy of Allan Button and Joan Reinert Button.)

Albert Reinert and Charles Button were in the high school band together. Their fathers, Edward Reinert and George Button, had floats in the same parade. The pioneer families celebrated the wedding of Joan Reinert, granddaughter of Edward, and Allan Button, grandson of George, on September 30, 1961. Pictured here are Joan and her brother Richard. (Courtesy of Allan Button and Joan Reinert Button.)

Four

PHYSICAL CHORES
IN THE HOMES, ON THE FIELDS, AND
BY THE LAKE

Chapter four gives a look at the work, occupations, physical chores, and tools that were required at Geneva Lake in the late 1800s and early 1900s. The chores depict labor that was required to keep up a household, raise a family, build a community, and retain a lifestyle. The work was physical and laborious. Some families were wealthy enough to have servants, some associations shared the maids and cooks, but the majority of women did their own household chores.

Housework alone was arduous and physical—cooking was performed on wood-burning or coal stoves, which caused soot and smoke to cover the walls. Lanterns and kerosene lamps also contributed to house soot, which required vigorous cleaning.

Regular cleaning consisted of beating rugs, scrubbing floors, sweeping porches, hand washing windows, and gardening without many tools. Laundry consisted of soaking the clothes in buckets, scrubbing them on rough washboards, rinsing, and wringing prior to outside hanging. The clothes were then pressed with flatirons and men's shirt collars stiffened with starch.

Preparing food was another task that required hard work and time. The cows had to be milked, and the poultry was bought alive or raised in the yard and required killing and plucking prior to cooking. Green coffee had to be roasted and ground, sugar was pounded, and flour was sifted. Vegetables were planted and harvested.

The photographs in this chapter are of servants and family women, as well as field-, railroad, and icehouse workers. Farmers, blacksmiths, and construction workers of Westgate Estate are also highlighted. Many of the pictures are of church fundraisers from the United Church of Christ (Congregational) of Williams Bay.

The United Church of Christ (Congregational) of Williams Bay, began in 1895 when a group of Williams Bay residents wanted to form an English-speaking church as the Free Evangelical Lutheran Church services alternated between the Swedish and Norwegian languages. With the help of the Ladies Aid Society, called the "Willing Workers," the first church was built in 1901. After fire destroyed the first church in 1911, funds were needed to rebuild. The women of the church did chores for $1 to help fund the reconstructing of their church. In 1912, the second church was erected.

Pictured here in 1912 is a blacksmith tending to the needs of horses in Williams Bay. The village of Fontana also had blacksmith stables. Horses were a large part of the lake during this time period and many famous horses were housed in the area. (Courtesy of the Barrett Memorial Library.)

Working as a blacksmith was hard and hot work, but necessary because the major type of transportation in the 1850s was horse and buggy, riding horseback, or boating. Of course, there was also walking and bicycling. (Courtesy of Donald Kemmett.)

Whether working in the home, on a job, or with a trade, work was laborious and very physical. Some of the work was a family affair, and children helped in the field or in the household along with the adults. (Courtesy of the Barrett Memorial Library.)

Firemen are ready for work in front of the Williams Bay fire station in 1928. Since many of the buildings were made of wood or had wood structures, fires were frequent. (Courtesy of Jim Moeller.)

In 1870, entrepreneurs took advantage of the clear ice resource from the lake. Ice harvesting became an important winter activity. The ice was stored in many layers of straw for insulation and was kept through the summer months for delivery to homes. (Courtesy of Allan Button and Joan Reinert Button.)

Boyle's icehouse, in 1907, employed 75 men to scrape, mark, cut, and deliver the ice to the chutes. Men then packed the ice to be shipped. Visible here is an icehouse that was started by Seymour. He shipped 10,000 tons of ice to Illinois annually. (Courtesy of Holly G. Starck.)

The mailman organizes the mail for delivery in Fontana. At first, it was delivered by horse and wagon, then by car, and much later by the mailboat. (Courtesy of Donald Kemmett.)

A female mail carrier in the early years delivers news to her customer. It is amazing to think women were working outside of the home in this generation. (Courtesy of Donald Kemmet.)

The back roads—in fact most roads—were not paved, and the town or village roads were mostly made of dirt. On most trips to Geneva Lake, and even around the lake, flat tires were not unusual and somewhat expected. (Courtesy of the United Church of Christ [Congregational] of Williams Bay, Phyllis Janda.)

When the businessmen would arrive by train from Chicago on a Friday afternoon, a steamboat or their own wooden boat would pick them up and deliver them to their summer home to relax and reengage with their families for the weekend. Pictured here is a worker who helps transport luggage for the train passengers. (Courtesy of the United Church of Christ [Congregational] of Williams Bay, Phyllis Janda.)

The first Geneva Lake area train service was established in the 1850s from Elgin, but only lasted four years. The Chicago & North Western Railway between Chicago, Lake Geneva, and Williams Bay began in the 1880s. (Courtesy of the Barrett Memorial Library.)

Conductors stand in front of the train in Williams Bay in the 1930s. The Irish immigrants laid the railroad. They bought land for their homes on Highway 50, which became known as the Irish Woods, and Woods School was created to provide schooling for Irish children. (Courtesy of Jim Moeller.)

Westgate was a granite English manor–style estate designed by British architect Clement B. Brun. Gertrude E. Allen commissioned this estate in 1917, after her father Charles, owner of Central Leather Company (a tannery), fell to his death from a window ledge at Chicago's Drake Hotel. (Courtesy of Bart and Joan Love.)

The construction crew was assembled from different companies like Barker Lumber Company and Walworth Lumber Company. In 1918, prior to the home being completed, Gertrude married a reputed podiatrist, George Westgate. She died the following summer from influenza while vacationing in New York and never lived in the home. (Courtesy of Bart and Joan Love.)

Westgate had many unique features, including an inglenook (a room for dining by an open fireplace), a basement with a bowing alley, billiards, and hobby room. In 1940, George subdivided the property and the main estate was sold to Pisors, who created a replica dollhouse called Westgate II, now preserved at the Webster House Museum. (Courtesy of Bart and Joan Love.)

A cross was designed in Westgate's stone gate wall to honor a worker who lost his eye in an accident during construction. Pictured here is Marie Pisor, the second owner of Westgate. She initiated the building of the Westgate replica dollhouse in 1979. It was completed in 1981. Photographs of the house were done by Duncan Fleming so the exact details of the Westgate could be re-created in the dollhouse. An eight-foot-long, five-and-a-half-foot-wide, and four-and-a-half-foot-high shell was built, and Mrs. Pisor did all the finishing touches to make the replica "real and true" to Westgate, both on the inside and outside. (Courtesy of Bart and Joan Love.)

Men are visible working on a wooden yacht. These yachts were used for transportation to and from the train station as well as for pleasure when cruising the lake. Wishing they could ride one of the yachts carrying wealthier summer visitors or in their own boat, Fritz and Allan Button used to watch the boats with envy. They bought a Grumann canoe with their summer earnings. Fritz became an expert iceboat designer, builder, and racer; and Allan became an expert canoe designer, builder, and racer. (Courtesy of Holly G. Starck.)

A man stores his boat in a field for the season. All the piers were removed from the lake prior to winter and stored in various locations, many times in the front yards of the homes facing the lake. The boats were moved to a storage facility or a boathouse, but they would reappear on the lake in spring for the summer months. (Courtesy of the United Church of Christ [Congregational] of Williams Bay, Phyllis Janda.)

The Lake Geneva area had a lot of farming. Hay was used in the barns and as horse feed. Dan Patch was a famous racehorse, owned briefly by Manley E. Sturges of New York and housed in the John J. Mitchell farm on the south shore of Lake Geneva. He made his big run at the Minnesota State Fair in 1908. (Courtesy of the United Church of Christ [Congregational] of Williams Bay, Phyllis Janda.)

An early tractor and a homemade wooden utility wagon were typical farm equipment. Once the men got out of the field, it was often the women's job to prepare what was harvested. (Courtesy of Allan Button and Joan Reinert Button.)

Grocery stores were really primitive. Waiting in line at the store was time-consuming for both the clerks and the shoppers. Groceries were commonly charged by the month. A home grocery delivery happened mostly by horse and wagon. Many got their food off the fields or from the chicken coops. (Courtesy of the United Church of Christ [Congregational] of Williams Bay, Phyllis Janda.)

A woman is milking her cow. Cows needed to be milked two to three times a day. Many farmers grew their own cow feed such as alfalfa, hay, and corn. Dairy farmers either leased or owned pastures for the livestock to graze. (Courtesy of the United Church of Christ [Congregational] of Williams Bay, Phyllis Janda.)

Here is a woman churning the milk to make cream and butter. With constant churning, the fat globules from the milk eventually form solid butter. (Courtesy of the United Church of Christ [Congregational] of Williams Bay, Phyllis Janda.)

A common occurrence was a homemaker, or a maid working while caring for a child. Pictured here is a woman with a child, making Wisconsin cheese. A section in the township of Linn was known as Linton. It was referred to as Slopville, because the cheese factory used to dump the whey in a meadow. Every Wisconsin book needs a cheese picture. (Courtesy of the United Church of Christ [Congregational] of Williams Bay, Phyllis Janda.)

After much of the work was done in the fields or with the farm animals, the next step was to gather the goods and take them out of the field, off the farm, or out of the coops so the food items could reach the families. (Courtesy of the United Church of Christ [Congregational] of Williams Bay, Phyllis Janda.)

Working on the farm was not the end of the workday. After harvesting the produce from the farm, the goods had to be delivered. Here, a woman and man deliver goods after working on the farm. (Courtesy of the United Church of Christ [Congregational] of Williams Bay, Phyllis Janda.)

A woman, with a child's help, is washing outside windows. Windows were plentiful because the owners wanted to see the views of the lake, fields, gardens, or trees. They also wanted the fresh air. (Courtesy of the United Church of Christ [Congregational] of Williams Bay, Phyllis Janda.)

Screens were put in the windows during the spring months. An attraction of lake living was getting the cool breeze off the lake during the hot summer season. Without air-conditioning, windows and open porches were an important aspect of staying cool. (Courtesy of the United Church of Christ [Congregational] of Williams Bay, Phyllis Janda.)

Many times, dishes were washed outside. Water mostly had to come from springs that were located a distance from the homes. Here are two women washing and drying the dishes outside. (Courtesy of the United Church of Christ [Congregational] of Williams Bay, Phyllis Janda.)

Washing clothes had many steps. First, they had to be soaked and then scrubbed against a washboard. Next, the clothes were rung by hand and hung to dry. Two women are visible washing clothes with fresh springwater. (Courtesy of the United Church of Christ [Congregational] of Williams Bay, Phyllis Janda.)

A maid is hanging clothing and other laundry to dry on an outdoor clothesline. The work was made more challenging on a windy day by the lake. (Courtesy of the United Church of Christ [Congregational] of Williams Bay, Phyllis Janda.)

Clothes are fresh off the line ready to be folded. These clothes were then taken into the residence to be placed or hung in their proper spot. Men's shirts had to have their collars ironed prior to being folded. The irons were held over a hot fire or placed on a woodstove to get heated. (Courtesy of the United Church of Christ [Congregational] of Williams Bay, Phyllis Janda.)

It was not uncommon to have hair washed and cut on the lawn outdoors. This is a man getting his hair washed in a bowl of springwater by a housekeeper. (Courtesy of the United Church of Christ [Congregational] of Williams Bay, Phyllis Janda.)

Vera is giving her son Scott a bath and washing his hair on the pier. Even if the photographs were not perfectly framed, a little off center, or blurred, they were still saved, put in scrapbooks, and cherished. (Courtesy of Leitner family.)

Even though there may have been some barbershops, it was just as convenient and common to have a housekeeper cut hair. Barbers use to be called barber-surgeons. Visible here, a housekeeper is cutting a man's hair in the backyard. Many got their haircut with lake views. (Courtesy of the United Church of Christ [Congregational] of Williams Bay, Phyllis Janda.)

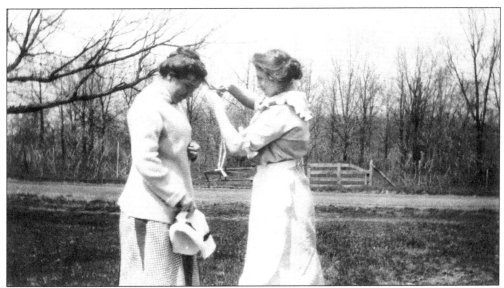

A maid is trimming a lady's hair prior to her going to a social function. The work of the maid was often preparing the lady of the house to attend formal functions. (Courtesy of the United Church of Christ [Congregational] of Williams Bay, Phyllis Janda.)

A man and woman prepare to do work in the garden. This was done with very few and, certainly by today's standards very primitive, tools. (Courtesy of the United Church of Christ [Congregational] of Williams Bay, Phyllis Janda.)

Much of the work in the garden was done by hand. This photograph is of a woman working in the garden weeding or planting on a spring day. (Courtesy of the United Church of Christ [Congregational] of Williams Bay, Phyllis Janda.)

A woman is raking fall leaves with a farmer and his wife looking on. The lake area was full of many different types of trees. Williams Bay and Fontana were referred to as having rugged rural forests, while the city of Lake Geneva was considered a developed community in the later 1800s. (Courtesy of the United Church of Christ [Congregational] of Williams Bay, Phyllis Janda.)

The land needed much work prior to planting. Here is a woman preparing her garden. (Courtesy of the United Church of Christ [Congregational] of Williams Bay, Phyllis Janda.)

Sweeping and cleaning were daily chores. Two women are preparing to do their work. (Courtesy of the United Church of Christ [Congregational] of Williams Bay, Phyllis Janda.)

A maid is visible cleaning the rug by sweeping it. Although this was years ago, in the early 1900s, the brooms, although primitive, have not changed a lot since. (Courtesy of the United Church of Christ [Congregational] of Williams Bay, Phyllis Janda.)

A housekeeper is beating the rug clean. Cleaning had to be done frequently because of the dirt and soot created by kerosene lights and fireplaces. (Courtesy of the United Church of Christ [Congregational] of Williams Bay, Phyllis Janda.)

A maid is sweeping a large rug outside the home. Much of the housework, such as cleaning or beating rugs, was done outside in the mid-1800s and early 1900s. (Courtesy of the United Church of Christ [Congregational] of Williams Bay, Phyllis Janda.)

A woman is sewing outdoors. Sewing clothes and repairing linens were part of the daily work. (Courtesy of the United Church of Christ [Congregational] of Williams Bay, Phyllis Janda.)

Here is another example of a women sewing. Making or repairing clothes was usually part of the woman's or the housekeeper's work. (Courtesy of the United Church of Christ [Congregational] of Williams Bay, Phyllis Janda.)

A maid is preparing to go shopping while a man window shops at the local bakery in Williams Bay. Part of the maid's job was to buy and prepare the food as well as do the clean up after the meal was finished. (Courtesy of the United Church of Christ [Congregational] of Williams Bay, Phyllis Janda.)

Getting water from the springs or from a well was a task. Many of the wells were not located close to the home. A maid is seen in this photograph pumping water that is located close to the home, which was not always the case. (Courtesy of the United Church of Christ [Congregational] of Williams Bay, Phyllis Janda.)

This is a woman mowing the yard. She appears to have a newer piece of equipment—a primitive lawn mower. (Courtesy of the United Church of Christ [Congregational] of Williams Bay, Phyllis Janda.)

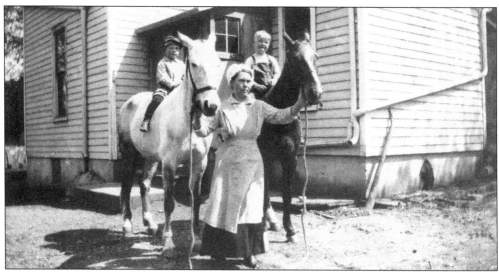

A maid or nanny is pictured caring for children. Keeping children entertained and busy was always part of the nanny's job. (Courtesy of the United Church of Christ [Congregational] of Williams Bay, Phyllis Janda.)

A maid is babysitting children by the Congress Club. Each club member could bring one maid to the association, and the club hired the other servants. The servants' quarters were above the dining facility. When the servants asked if they could bathe in the lake, they were denied the privilege. (Courtesy of the United Church of Christ [Congregational] of Williams Bay, Phyllis Janda.)

A typical image of the time was that of a farmer with his family after a day's work. Hay had to be unbundled for the horses, and fields had to be seeded, harvested, and plowed. A farmer's work was never really done, but one of the rewards of all the work was coming home to a family in the evening. (Courtesy of the United Church of Christ [Congregational] of Williams Bay, Phyllis Janda.)

The churchwomen performed household duties for a dollar, raising funds to rebuild their church that had burned. The United Church of Christ (Congregational) of Williams Bay was rebuilt and dedicated on May 19, 1912. In the late 1800s, church services in Williams Bay were only in Swedish and Norwegian. These are two women are displaying their earned fundraising dollar. (Courtesy of the United Church of Christ [Congregational] of Williams Bay, Phyllis Janda.)

The United Church of Christ (Congregational) of Williams Bay began in 1895 when a group of Williams Bay residents wanted to form an English-speaking church, as the Free Evangelical Lutheran Church services alternated between Swedish and Norwegian languages. With the help of the Ladies Aid Society, called the "Willing Workers," the first church was built in 1901. After fire destroyed the first church in 1911, a second church was built on the site in 1912 (pictured). (Courtesy of the United Church of Christ [Congregational] of Williams Bay, Phyllis Janda.)

Five

PLAYFULNESS AND PEACEFULNESS
SAILING, SWIMMING, FISHING, GOLFING, BOATING, AND MORE

The last chapter illustrates what attracted individuals and families to the lake and why they kept coming back. The activities are year-round, which makes Geneva Lake a destination for all seasons. The activities, coupled with the lake's beauty and sense of community, make it a very special vacation spot or place to live for all ages. This chapter illustrates the dress, style, fun, and formality of individuals and families in the late 1800s and early 1900s.

Perhaps the simplest yet most magical activity at the lake is walking the shore path in all seasons. The 21-mile lakeshore path is opened year-round to all. Ever since Indians inhabited the lake with a walkway, there has been a lakeshore path right-of-way for the public that was made perpetual in 1833. Property owners are required to maintain their sections of path for pedestrians. Some individuals walk the entire path at one time, others divide the shore path in sections, and yet others repeat their favorite shore path walk on a regular basis—alone or with friends and family.

The things-to-do list at the lake has never really changed through the decades. The equipment, dress, and comfort may have improved, but individuals and families generally still spend time doing the same activities that their grandparents and great-grandparents did years ago. Perhaps this is one attraction to the lake: a connection to families past.

Swimming, sunbathing, sailing, touring in steamboats, riding in speedboats, iceboats, and canoes were popular. Water- and snow skiing, sleighing, ice-skating, and ice hockey were also accessible. Locals enjoyed fishing and hunting. Fishing was on open lake water or from huts on the ice.

Golf, tennis, croquet, archery, paddle tennis, and bridge were other activities that individuals spent their time playing. Breeding as well as riding horses also flourished.

Most of the activities were for one's leisurely pleasure, but some like sailing, iceboating, golfing, playing tennis, and bridge were very competitive and produced local, national, and international champions. Of course, there are also photographs of individuals, families, and friends just relaxing, reading, or reflecting in this peaceful lake environment.

Geneva Lake had year-round activities. From winter to summer, families could spend time outside enjoying what the lake had to offer. Some of the early recreational activities included fishing, sailing, swimming, hunting, golfing, ice-skating, ice hockey, iceboating, and ice fishing. (Courtesy of Curt Carlson.)

Jody Pollock (Pringle) is spending time outdoors as a young child. She is enjoying the lake's winter weather at Rainbow Point. Jody, after sifting through photographs to contribute to this book, is convinced her grandchildren need to organize the images into scrapbooks for future generations to enjoy and appreciate. (Courtesy of Jody Pringle.)

Marcella and Mary Anne Niehoff (Kirchschlager) are sleighing in 1938. Loyola University Chicago School of Nursing is named after Marcella Niehoff. She was active in supporting the Holiday Home Camp, which was created in 1886 to give underprivileged Chicago children a lake experience. Lake Geneva Fresh Air Association was formed to support this charity and other community efforts. (Courtesy of Mary Anne Kirchschlager.)

A homemade rigged-up form of an iceboat is visible in the early 1920s in Williams Bay. Over 18,000 years ago, glaciers formed this 152-foot-deep, spring-fed, crystal-clear inland lake. When the lake was frozen, cars, horses, fishing huts, and skaters were seen on the ice. (Courtesy of Jim Moeller.)

Williams Bay is considered the iceboating capital of the world. The wind, ice, and weather have to come together to get a perfect day for iceboating. The wind has to be strong, the ice has to be thickly frozen, and snow has to be minimal. Sylvester Beers is visible here racing *I 186*. (Courtesy of Steve Beers.)

Iceboating was just not for boys. Pictured in 1915 are iceboaters Ella Butler Monson and Bella Monson Hart. (Courtesy of Bonnie Cornue.)

Showing off the catch has always been half the fun of fishing. Fish that can be found in the lake include bluegill, brook trout, brown trout, lake trout, largemouth bass, northern pike, rainbow trout, smallmouth bass, slake, and walleye. (Courtesy of Bonnie Cornue.)

Fishing was done for sport, food, and income. Both ice fishing with a hut or fishing open water in a boat or on a pier were always popular. "Ciscoes are running" was the signal for the gathering of fisherman on the lake, since the catch would be good. Pictured is four-year-old Phyllis Killar (Janda) after catching her first bass at Conference Point Shores. (Courtesy of Phyllis Janda.)

113

Vince and Jozephine Sorren were honeymooning in 1942 when they shot this photograph of a water safety patrol boat on Buttons Bay. They both loved Geneva Lake, and in 1955, they realized their honeymoon dream and bought a home in Trinke Estates. Water safety in both winter and summer is a priority. (Courtesy of Vince and Nona Sorren.)

Dave Moeller, from Williams Bay, owned the boat named *Fannie May*. Originally owned by the Chicago-based Fannie May Candy Company, it was used for racing. The transportation company charged 25¢ per 25 miles for a boat ride. (Courtesy of Jim Moeller.)

These boaters have finished rowing and are being towed in by an uncle. Note the writing on the photograph to capture the memories. This is how most scrapbooks were documented so future generations would know who was in the picture. (Courtesy of Bonnie Cornue.)

The lake was home to families from different spheres of life. The summer people lived in mansions, cottages, or tents. The locals provided supplies, food, and services. The lake was an equalizer, as all individuals used it for transportation and pleasure. (Courtesy of Holly G. Stark.)

COLLEGE CAMP GOLF CLUB, Williams Bay, Wisconsin. (On Lake Geneva)   21704-4

College Camp next to Yerkes originally had a six-hole golf course that was started at the turn of the 20th century. It was expanded to 18 holes in 1918 by a gift from S.B. Chapin. (Courtesy of Martha Kiefer Cucco.)

Harry learned to golf from his father, Harry George Smeltzer Sr., when he was a high school student in Pennsylvania. Later, the majority of his golf was played in the Geneva Lake area with his daughter. He golfed at all three clubs— Geneva National Golf Club, Lake Geneva Country Club, and Big Foot Country Club. He scored 93 during his last round of golf. (Courtesy of Carolyn Hope Smeltzer.)

On December 30, 1895, a meeting was held in Chicago to discuss the consideration of plans for a country Club in Lake Geneva. The first Lake Geneva Country Club's clubhouse burned and was replaced with a building designed by Robert B. Spencer Jr. and built by Reinert and Malsch. (Courtesy of Holly G. Starck.)

Mary A. Kelly is ready to putt. She brought her family for summer vacations to stay in the icehouse of the Brookwood Estate. Colonel Parker, Elvis Presley's famous manager, stayed at Brookwood Estate in the mid-1950s. That summer, Elvis called the Colonel in Lake Geneva many times. This story of Elvis was recounted by Bill Jacobs. (Courtesy of Bob Kelly and Carolyn Hope Smeltzer.)

Mary Anne Niehoff (Kirchschlager), at her Towering Elms estate, is posing with two unidentified young men prior to practicing archery. The estate had elm trees on the property that fell victim to Dutch elm disease. One of the trees fell on, and destroyed, the guesthouse. (Courtesy of Mary Anne Kirchschlager.)

Croquet was a common game in the lake area. Often, all the players were dressed in white. Here, players pose for a photograph before starting their game of croquet on the lakefront property of Rainbow Point during the 1920s. (Courtesy of Jody Pringle.)

A tennis match is in action. Many of the estates had their own tennis courts. (Courtesy of Sharon O'Brien.)

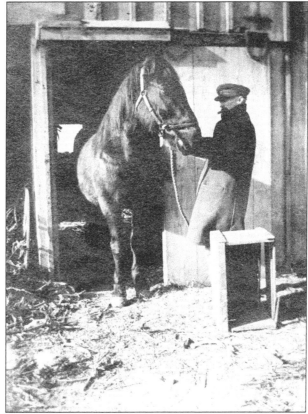

The world-champion trotter Lou Delbon was from the C.K.G. Billings farm. A.G. Harris, son of Norman Harris, raised horses at the Kemah Farm. His will directed his horses be buried on the property, and when building Geneva National, horses were found buried on the grounds and had to be relocated. This image illustrates caring for horses. (Courtesy of Bonnie Cornue.)

Horse racing was not just a summer sport. Elmer Zingle, president of the Lake Geneva Harness Association, promoted horse racing on the ice. His horse was Sailor Boy. Zingle was also chairperson of Operation Snowman, which organized a toboggan slide going onto the lake from Library Park. This photograph was taken by E.G. Eisner. (Courtesy of Joan Eisner Miller.)

In 1893, the World's Columbian Exposition artifacts and building were brought to the Geneva Lake area along with some of the first Arabian horses in the area. Harris started the first Arabian Horse Registry in America and became its first president. The Mid Summer Fair at the Leiter estate in 1905 is visible here. (Courtesy of Holly G. Starck.)

Edward Gustav Uihlein and August Manns Uihlein, with their daughter, Melita (later Mrs. William Seipp) are at their home known as Forest Glen. The house design was by Henry Lord Gay, modified by Emil Fromann, and the landscape design was by Jens Jensen. On Sundays, the public was invited to enjoy their gardens. The photograph was provided with courtesy of a great-grandson of the Uihleins. (Courtesy of John K. Notz Jr.)

The shore path, first established by the Indians, provided a passageway between the encampments. Lakefront landowners at various times attempted to block access of the shore path. They were not legally successful due to the "right of prescription" as the precedent of open access had already been established in 1883. (Courtesy of Barrett Memorial Library.)

The 21-mile footpath around the lake was not uniform. Each homeowner maintained his portion of the path. Giant willows, elms, maples, and oaks lined the path that was made of dirt, stone, brick, or wood. Often, a rest was needed when walking the shore path. (Courtesy of Courtesy of Barrett Memorial Library.)

Pictured here is the shore path bridge in Fontana. Elaborate gardens could be viewed when walking the path. Frank Button, a greenhouse owner, stated some of the shore path's flower beds stretched over half a mile, and there seemed to always be a rose garden. (Courtesy of Jody Pringle.)

In 1872, Kaye's Park was a south shore resort with a farm, built on 300 acres. Later, it became the property of the Northwestern Academy. Katherine Nohelty (second from left) and friends are visible resting at the Northwestern Academy. Katherine, a 1937 graduate of Loyola's law school, was the first woman elected as a municipal court judge in Chicago. (Courtesy of Mary Ann McDermott.)

Grace, Florence, Camil, and Grace are posing in front of the Geneva Lake in Williams Bay. They are bathing beauties in this 1922 image. The lake is 5,500 acres, three miles wide, and nine miles long. (Courtesy of Curt Carlson.)

Bathing beauties are visible here at all ages. Three generations of a family are enjoying the lake and showing off their swimming suits in 1926. Time spent together at the lake was precious. Memories were captured in photographs and put into scrapbooks. (Courtesy of Bonnie Cornue.)

John Haverson, editor of the *Lake Geneva Regional News*, wrote an article requesting vintage photographs and stories for this book, *Geneva Lake*, in the late summer of 2013. Within two months, the authors collected over 800 photographs with stories. The pictures came from Illinois, Minnesota, Nebraska, and Wisconsin. Contributors gave between one and 100 photographs each. This made the photograph and story selection process difficult for the authors but reinforced the sentiment that individuals wanted their families and memories to be part of history. (Courtesy of Curt Carlson.)

This image shows someone about to dive into Geneva Lake in Williams Bay. The authors hope the readers enjoyed "diving" into this vintage scrapbook, which was made up of historical photographs and personal family stories. The authors and the readers owe one big thank-you to the community that cares about, and contributed to, Geneva Lake history. (Courtesy of Curt Carlson.)

Having lake fun at the Williams Bay bathhouse are Frank Jr. (left) and Laddie Fleishman with an unidentified child. This photograph, from Filimena Fleishman Killar's album *Williams Bay Family Summers at the Cottage from 1927–1952*, is typical of those shown in *Geneva Lake* as it was taken out of a family scrapbook. The authors hope that they have inspired the readers to organize their own forms of scrapbooks so future generations can enjoy their family histories. (Courtesy of Phyllis Janda.)

George Kiefer is sailing on Geneva Lake. He spent summers at Lake Geneva with his family. He was a renowned sailor, winning many races. George's daughter Martha follows in his footsteps and enjoys sailing today on Geneva Lake. (Courtesy of Martha Kiefer Cucco.)

Harry Smeltzer, pictured on his 1940 Chevy, received a Purple Heart for his service as a sailor on the USS *Franklin* (CV-13), during World War II. While living in Indiana, he and his wife, Mary, vacationed in Williams Bay. It was there he played golf with his daughter Carolyn, who is an avid golfer. (Courtesy of Carolyn Hope Smeltzer.)

BIBLIOGRAPHY

Colwell, Authur Sr., MD. *History of the Big Foot Country Club and the Territory at the West End of Geneva Lake*. Walworth, WI: Walworth/Fontana Times Reporter, 1964.

Denison, Bonnie Burton. *Picturesque Lake Geneva*. Lake Geneva, WI: Wisconsin Transportation Company, 1926.

Franzene, Jessica. "Elgin on the Shore: From Camp to Club, an Association's Lakeside History." *Welcome Home Newspaper*, 2013.

"In the Good OL Summer Time," The Annals of Congress Club. Inc., 1882 . . . 1982, A Century of Julys and Augusts. Lake Geneva, WI: Congress Club, 1982.

Jenkins, Paul. *The Book of Lake Geneva*. Chicago: University of Chicago Press, 1924.

Kutchai, Elizabeth "Libby" Probasco. Letter to the editor. *Lake Geneva Regional News*, 2010.

Livingston, Martha, W. *Hickory Hut, Life at Rockford Camp on Geneva Lake Beginning in 1910*.

Manierre, George. "Early Recollections of Lake Geneva (Big Foot Lake), Wisconsin." *Wisconsin Magazine of History* vol. 1, no. 2.

Miller, Pi (Margaret Louise). *History of the Leonard family at Rockford Camp 1890–2000*.

Miller, Sumner. *Rockford Camp, Lake Geneva "In the Good Old Summer Time,"* 1935.

Nohelty, Katherine. *School Girl Days, A Memory Book*. Lake Geneva, WI: Lake Geneva High School, 1918.

Park, Margaret Smith. "History of 100 Years of Belvidere Park Recalled." *Times*, 1975.

Smeltzer, Carolyn and Martha Cucco. *Lake Geneva in Vintage Postcards*. Charleston, SC: Arcadia Publishing, 2005.

United Church of Christ (Congregational) of Williams Bay. *Celebrating 100 Years of Church Family, 1896–1996*.

Von Biesbroeck, Mrs. George. *History of Williams Bay*, 1957.

Willis, Terri. *The Geneva Inn, A History of the Property*. Lake Geneva, WI: Geneva Inn, 2013.

Carolyn Hope Smeltzer is seen reading at a very young age, with her parents, Mary and Harry. Martha Kiefer (Cucco) is ready to perform.

Visit us at
arcadiapublishing.com

CPSIA information can be obtained
at www.ICGtesting.com
Printed in the USA
BVHW091641151221
624010BV00006B/1316